A Transport Travelogue
by road, rail and water, 1948-1972

Part 3, Eastern and Midland Counties: Norfolk to Cheshire

Cedric Greenwood

First published in 2018

British Library Cataloguing in Publication Data

A catalogue record for this book is available from the British Library.

ISBN 978 1 85794 504 1

Silver Link Publishing Ltd
The Trundle
Ringstead Road
Great Addington
Kettering
Northants NN14 4BW

Tel/Fax: 01536 330588
email: sales@nostalgiacollection.com
Website: www.nostalgiacollection.com

Printed and bound in the Czech Republic

Some of the pictures in this book appeared previously in the same author's *Merseyside: The Indian Summer* (Silver Link Publishing, 2007) and *Echoes of Steam and Vintage Voltage* (Silver Link Publishing, 2015).

Acknowledgements

My thanks for making this series of books possible go to those who printed my black and white photographs: Ian Breckin of Silvertone, Leeds; Steve Howe of the Black & White Picture Place, Chester; and the late Ken Tyhurst of Canterbury.

Thanks also to those who processed my colour slides and prints: Fujifilm laboratories, Warwick; and CC Imaging Photo Lab, Leeds.

In writing the introductory text and captions I am indebted to the following people for information and assistance: Roy Andrews, berthing manager, Mersey Docks; Ted Gadsby of Walsall, regarding old buses and buildings in Birmingham and Wednesbury; Steven Hannibal, Network Rail, local operations manager at Boston; the late Bruce Maund of Birkenhead, transport historian; Glynn Parry of Bromborough, local history lecturer; Pat Rudrum of Holt, Norfolk, my Internet intermediary; Tom Turner of Wallasey for help in identifying and dating motor vehicles; and Danny Witherington of British Waterways' north-west office, Wigan.

I am also indebted for information to the staff of Mersey Ferries, Seacombe; National Waterways Museum, Ellesmere Port; New Holland Bulk Services; Norfolk County Libraries, for computer services at Holt; and Peel Ports (Mersey Marine Section).

Title page: **BUXTON** Among the properly dressed promenaders in The Crescent on 22 April 1962 we see a Silver Cross pram and a 1957 model of the 1949-style Ford Anglia car, both in black. Dark grey stonework, iron and glass colonnades and landscaped parkland are characteristic features of this hilly spa town. At just over 1,000 feet, Buxton is the highest town in England and, like Bath, has been a spa since Roman times. The building on the left is the north end of The Crescent, a Georgian leisure centre with assembly rooms and accommodation for visitors to St Ann's Well. Next is the Cavendish Arcade of shops built around a thermal bath of 1854. Buxton now has nine springs of warm, pale-blue mineral water that gush from 3,500 to 5,000 feet below ground in this limestone country.

Right: **SEACOMBE** In the mid-20th century Merseyside was the biggest flour milling centre in Europe and second in the world after Minneapolis in the North American prairies. Grain arrived by ship from North and South America, Australia, India and Europe. Here we see ships berthed at the giant granaries and mills on the Wallasey side of the East Float at Seacombe on 22 October 1962. From the left are the Belgian ship *Schelde* at Buchanan's mills, dating from 1893, two smoking J. H. Lamey tugs lying alongside the Irish ship *Irish Rowan* at Paul Brothers' Homepride Mills, a third Lamey tug by the old granary of 1868, and a third grain freighter at the colossal new concrete grain silo belonging to the Liverpool Grain Store & Transit Company. We can also see Alfred Dock drawbridge raised and part of another ship loading at Vittoria Wharf, Birkenhead, on the right.

Contents

Introduction

This is an interesting east-west journey across the breadth of England from the cornfields and skylarks of Norfolk to the smokestacks and cranes on the Cheshire bank of the Mersey. Cross-country journeys like this are slow and difficult because all main roads and railways radiate from London across our path – but it was easier between 1893 and 1959 thanks to the **Midland & Great Northern Joint Railway** and its successors the LMS&LNEJR, which gave us direct trains from east Norfolk to Spalding, Peterborough, Leicester, Birmingham, Manchester and Liverpool and through carriages to Lowestoft and Southport.

The Midland Railway extended its line from Leicester east from Little Bytham in Lincolnshire while the Great Northern shot out a branch north-east from Peterborough, the two lines converging at Sutton Bridge in the Lincolnshire fens. Together they pushed on to King's Lynn, where they joined up with a combination of Norfolk railway enterprises to complete a through line east across Norfolk, through Great Eastern Railway territory, to the east coast. The route over upland Norfolk between the Broads and the Fens is pleasantly rolling and wooded, rising to 316 feet between Thursford and Melton Constable. At Melton the lines fanned out to Great Yarmouth, Norwich and Cromer. The main line featured long steel bridges across the Great Ouse at King's Lynn and Breydon Water near Great Yarmouth.

When the railways were grouped in 1923 the M&GNJR became the LMS&LNEJR, but the rundown began in 1936, when it passed entirely to the LNER, although the LMSR generated most of the passengers and freight. The LNER began closing down the workshops at Melton Constable and moving the work to Stratford and elsewhere. On nationalisation in 1948 the network was in BR's Eastern Region and this cross-country facility ended in 1959 with the closure of 180 miles of main lines across Norfolk and Lincolnshire including Great Yarmouth and Norwich (except for short freight workings near King's Lynn and Norwich, the last of which was withdrawn in 1982). Oddly enough, the 15-mile branch line from Melton Constable to Cromer stayed open for passengers for another five years (pictured), then closed as far as Sheringham in 1964, leaving the current Cromer-Sheringham section as an extension of the Network Rail line from Norwich to Cromer. Today the 6-mile Sheringham-Holt section is the privately preserved and prestigious North Norfolk Railway, the 'Poppy Line'.

The railway created the village of **Melton Constable** and the uniformity of this small grid of plain, stern, uniform, terraced houses marks it out as a railway village, looking like part of a midland industrial town set incongruously in rural Norfolk. This four-way railway junction was the site of the M&GNJR's main loco shed and workshops and the reason for the creation and existence of the village as we know it today. The railway company built 99 houses in Melton and provided the water works, sewage works, gas works, school, mission hall, institute, bowling green, tennis courts and the corrugated iron church. The coming of the railway saw the population of this rural parish rise from 118 in 1881 to 1,157 in 1911. The size of the village doubled with an extended grid of private terraced houses; nine out of ten residents worked for the railway, which employed nearly 1,000 people at Melton in its heyday, many of them coming from neighbouring villages. Melton was the home of William Marriott, the company's engineer (1883-1924), locomotive superintendent (1884-1924) and traffic manager (1919-24). He was the patriarch of the village, supervising improvement classes for engineering and operating staff in the Railway Institute, and village life was regulated by the works hooter.

Melton Constable station consisted of a 260-yard-long island platform between the east and west junctions where trains met and divided three ways. North of it was the goods yard and south of it were the engine shed and turntable, the erecting shop where locomotives were built, rebuilt and repaired, separate workshops for repairing and rebuilding carriages and wagons, a foundry, smithy, machine shop, boiler shop, joinery shop and paint shop. There were also workshops for making concrete lineside structures and wagon sheets. After the closure of the workshops there were still 250 railwaymen based at Melton when the main line closed in 1959.

Today it is hard to imagine that any of this was ever there. The large brick loco shed and workshops have been incorporated into a new industrial estate on the railway works site. The triple-section water tower is still there on the horizon and the Railway Institute is still the social centre. Bereft of its railway, Melton Constable's population had declined to 550 by the end of the 20th century and the village is now a sad ghost of its old self, its streets cluttered with parked cars, obstructing the passage of lorries on the main street, the B1354, serving the industrial estate. Despite its designation as a conservation area in 1990, Melton Constable has lost much of the neat uniformity of its frontages that was its distinctive feature.

The biggest monument to the M&GNJR is Cross Keys Bridge over the River Nene at Sutton Bridge, where the lines diverged to Peterborough and Leicester. This was a railway swing bridge, with a control cabin on top; the single-line railway shared the bridge with a single-lane carriageway controlled by signals. Now the railway has gone it's a two-way road bridge. The line to Peterborough went via Wisbech, which was also served by the GER, the two lines converging and diverging on opposite sides of the town without meeting.

Today Wisbech is bereft of railways. It also had a fascinating Dutch-type rural roadside steam tramway running 7½ miles south along the boundary between Norfolk and Cambridgeshire. It was a standard-gauge branch of the GER from Wisbech station to Upwell, and ran alongside the Wisbech Canal and Well Creek, which gave it even more of a Dutch character, together with the fen landscape. The **Wisbech & Upwell Tramway** terminated at Outwell in 1883 and Upwell in 1884 as a light railway to carry passengers and goods – mainly coal in and fruit and vegetables out – from the rich, black, fenland soil. Authorised under the 1870 Tramways Act, it ran unfenced along the roadside grass verge and crossed and re-crossed the road diagonally with no more protection than a red flag. The 0-4-0 and 0-6-0 steam tram engines looked like goods brake vans, with a cab and cowcatcher at each end and side valances as skirting over the wheels. They were interchangeable with similar ex-GER tram engines on street shunting duties at Colchester, Ipswich and Great Yarmouth. They were also the model for 'Toby the Tram Engine' in the children's books by the Rev Wilbert Awdry, vicar of nearby Emneth. The gaslit, four-wheel and bogie coaches had longitudinal seating, passengers boarded by the steps and veranda at each end, and the guard collected the fares en route.

The passenger service ended in 1927 but the line was still carrying coal, fruit, vegetables and general goods when I cycled over to Wisbech and Upwell one day off in 1961 while I was on the staff at RAF Bircham Newton. It was a 35-mile cycle ride each way, but I arrived too late; I was disappointed to find that the motive power had been modernised in 1952 with 0-6-0 diesel shunters, though still with

cowcatchers fore and aft and skirting over the wheels. Thus, for me, the line had lost its attraction and I did not take any photographs. Seventy miles is a long way to cycle to see a diesel shunter but the right of way of the tramway was worth seeing. The line was closed in 1966 and the track lifted in 1968, but its route is traceable today and the line is fondly remembered locally and well illustrated in books. The coaches with verandas survived by further service on the LNER's Kelvedon & Tollesbury Light Railway in Essex until that closed in 1951. The two bogie coaches were saved: one was earmarked for the National Railway Museum but was inadvertently scrapped at Stratford Works, while the other was used in the film *The Titfield Thunderbolt* in 1952 and is now preserved on the North Norfolk Railway at Holt.

Norfolk once had a veritable network of railways to serve its farms, fishing ports and small seaside resorts, but most lines, including the M&GNJR main line, appeared to meander across the sparsely populated countryside in search of a terminus. Eight towns and villages had two stations on different lines – Thetford, Worstead, North Walsham, Aylsham, Reepham, Cromer, Fakenham and King's Lynn – while Great Yarmouth and Norwich each had three stations. I remember riding the 7½-mile **branch line from Denver to Stoke Ferry** in west Norfolk in about 1954, although the line closed to passengers in 1930. I was on a troop train and Stoke Ferry was the railhead for RAF Marham. The branch stayed open to Stoke Ferry for goods till 1965 and to Abbey station for sugar beet till 1982.

The village of **Burnham Market**, (page 17), was on the ex-GER West Norfolk branch from Heacham to Wells-next-the-Sea. Victorian locomotives pulled clerestory-roofed, gaslit carriages on this line right up to the end of passenger service in 1952. The North Sea coast floods in 1953 washed out the track across Holkham marsh on the way

to Wells, so Burnham became the terminus for the daily goods train for the last 11 years. The branch closed in 1964 together with its stem, King's Lynn-Hunstanton. Four of the six stations along the branch survive as private houses, three with platforms and one with its signal cabin. Burnham retains its buffer stop on a short track from its time as the terminus; it is now a guest house with a replica four-wheel coach for the guests, and Wells station is also a second-hand bookshop. This is typical of the survival rate of closed railway stations throughout Norfolk, and many old station houses survive on the former M&GNJR. Both sides of the ornate royal station at Wolferton (for Sandringham) on the closed King's Lynn-Hunstanton branch are private residences and have been beautifully restored together with the signal cabin, which is attached to a row of ornate railway cottages. The down side of the station, with a museum of railway artefacts, is often open to the public.

Most of Norfolk's railways closed in the 1950s – before Beeching – and by the mid-1960s there was a large blank on the railway map within the area bounded by Norwich, Sheringham, Ely and King's Lynn. The only cross-country route from Norfolk now is the through train service from Norwich to Liverpool, but it's a roundabout route, the train has to reverse at Ely and Sheffield, and the journey takes 6½ hours. The highlight of the route is the scenic section through the Pennines between Sheffield and Manchester, (page 36).

When I was on leave from RAF Bircham Newton in August 1961, I was booked by train from King's Lynn to Liverpool to stay bed and breakfast at New Brighton on the first night. My train from March to Peterborough East was running a few minutes late and I had only 12 minutes to change at Peterborough from the East station on the former Great Eastern to North station on the old Great Northern (these stations were actually south and west of the city respectively, but named after their original owners the GER and GNR). There were no cabs in sight so I had to run with my rucksack through crowded streets, but I missed my scheduled 'connection' at Peterborough by less than a minute. The next train to Liverpool was in 2 hours' time so I hitch-hiked.

It was quite easy **hitch-hiking** in those days before motorways and I had developed a good knowledge of the A class road system from experience. I hitched via the A47, the A5 and the A41 in five lifts and arrived at Birkenhead – more convenient for New Brighton – 18 minutes before the train I missed was due into Liverpool on the other side of the Mersey.

There was another time when hitch-hiking came in useful after missing a coach departure for a journey across the Midlands. On the last day of December 1965 I was booked by coach from London to Kendal but I'd dallied too long in a railway record shop in Islington and arrived at Victoria Coach Station just in time to see the convoy of Standerwick double-deck coaches (as seen on page 27) leaving the other end of the coach station. So I took a Standerwick timetable, went by underground train from Victoria to Hendon and thumbed lifts in two lorries and a car to Coventry, where I caught up with the Standerwicks in Pool Meadow bus station just 2 minutes before they were due to leave.

Back in the 1940s I became interested in tramcars as a result of several visits to Leicester, Dad's home town, to visit Grandpa and Grandma. Such was the state of security and trust in the post-war years that my solo travels began at the age of 10, in 1948, when I was given the freedom to ride **Leicester tramways** on my own for a day. Dad had a glass plate camera and one day I stood at his side when he took the two Leicester tramscapes for me that appear in these pages. The Corporation operated 178 tramcars of this standard design,

dating from 1904 to 1922. Four lines radiated from the Clock Tower leading to eight radial lines to the outskirts, with four belt lines linking the radial lines. Track, overhead and cars were well maintained, with improvements and extensions, the cars were fast, and services ran at intervals of every 3 to 7 minutes. After the war the track and cars were due for renewal and, as the suburbs spread outward, the ageing trams were replaced by cheaper new motorbuses between 1947 and 1949. This was the story of the demise of the surviving post-war tramways all over Britain, though some larger systems persevered, with new track and new cars, into the 1950s and '60s.

My favourite route across the Midlands was the Great Western's north main line from **Paddington to Birkenhead**, which crossed the province from Banbury General to Birkenhead Woodside. It was a much more interesting, scenic route than the LMSR from Euston via Rugby and Crewe. Fast through trains ran between Paddington and Birkenhead from 1861 to 1967. The first, on 1 October 1861, was the first standard-gauge train to leave Paddington, and on 7 March 1862 Britain's first corridor train entered service on this route. The original route was through the Thames valley via Reading and Oxford but the 1910 cut-off route through High Wycombe and the Chiltern Hills took 18¼ miles off the journey. The two lines converged on Banbury then headed north-west across the beautiful rolling, wooded country of Warwickshire and Shropshire and dipped into the Welsh hills via Wrexham on the way to Chester and the Wirral peninsula.

It was 210¼ miles from Paddington to Birkenhead by the direct route and, with 13 stops on the way, the journey took the best part of 6 hours. I rode this route each way between Oxford General and Birkenhead Woodside ten times a year from 1949 to 1952. There were stations and halts every 2 miles on average and I can still recite the

names of all 84 of them in sequence; many of them have closed since. Great Western stations were spacious with wide platforms and canopies and ample, architectural buildings in local stone, brick or timber with gas lamps, rock gardens and large, legible station nameboards with white cast-iron capital letters screwed on to black boards in white frames. Snow Hill station, Birmingham, rebuilt in 1906-11,

LEICESTER At the Clock Tower are tramcars in East Gates (foreground) and Haymarket (background). Here the A6 (London to Carlisle) trunk road, the A46 (Grimsby to Bath) and the A47 (Great Yarmouth to Birmingham) crossed each other, as indicated by the RAC road sign on the left.

The Clock Tower was also the hub of the Leicester tramway system, a complex web of tracks, with tramcars passing both ways on three sides of the Victorian Gothic clock tower of 1868 and radiating in three directions, along High Street (behind the camera), Humberstone Gate and Gallowtree Gate. A point duty policeman regulated the traffic at the pedestrian crossing in the foreground. Leicester had begun replacing tramcars with motorbuses but there were still 13 routes operating when this picture was taken in the summer of 1948 and there are three crimson and cream tramcars and a few motor vehicles in this picture, including a 1948 Austin removals van (right).

Only the clock tower and the buildings on the left survive today, but all the shops have changed owners and uses. The range of buildings across the background, including the White Hart Hotel, has been replaced by the stark, horizontal lines of a balconied, rectangular, modern shopping centre that appears to turn its back on its city centre location. The area has been repaved as part of the city centre pedestrian zone with restricted vehicular access.
George Greenwood

was particularly light, spacious and well appointed in the Edwardian idiom in contrast to the gloomy LMSR station at New Street. Shrewsbury station is like an Oxford college in Tudor brick and stonework, Gobowen is stuccoed Italianate, and Chester General is a cavernous, Italianate station with brick arcading. The country halts, on the other hand, were short, narrow wooden platforms with leaning nameboards, Spartan wooden shelters and a few oil lamps. All the halts have gone now; so too have the grand stations I knew at Birmingham Snow Hill and Birkenhead Woodside, which were demolished after the closure of this through route in 1967. Four stations on this route are illustrated in these pages. Owing to restrictive franchises and line closures, to follow this route closely today one would have to ride three multiple unit trains and one articulated tramcar from London Marylebone to Birkenhead Hamilton Square.

The 13 miles from Birmingham Snow Hill to Wolverhampton Low Level (now the route of the Midland Metro tramway) traversed the **Black Country** of south Staffordshire, so named from its smoky industries, based on the coal and iron mined there. It provided an interesting foil to the otherwise scenic rural route. There were nine stations in those 13 miles, with railway yards, rooftops, smokestacks and church steeples as far as the eye could see. I was fascinated by the fantastically weathered slag heaps and the fleeting image of a steaming, red canal alongside a steelworks. In the Black Country network of canals and railways there were several canal basins served by railway sidings.

Little is left of the once extensive labyrinth of canals and railways in the Black Country or the industries they served. Many of the extant small railway stations have been reduced to minimal facilities, often with no staff. Old Hill, pictured here, was the junction with the branches to Halesowen and Dudley. The Dudley branch was known locally

as the 'Bumble Hole'. All the stops had rather quaint names: Old Hill (High Street) Halt, Darby End Halt, Windmill End, Baptist End Halt and Blowers Green – this presumably a reference to glass blowing, an old Black Country industry, together with making chains, nails and tools. The Dudley branch closed to passengers in 1964 and to goods a few years later.

The Black Country also had the most intensive network of **broad and narrow canals** in Britain. This was the heart of the system of man-made waterways and canalised rivers that linked the Thames, Severn, Trent and Mersey, criss-crossing the midland counties, built mainly in the period 1770 to 1830. Before the coming of the railways these waterways carried all the commercial commodities generated by the Industrial Revolution and there were even 'fly packet boats' carrying passengers. Birmingham canals had many grim but picturesque 'noir' industrial scenes, which have all but disappeared with the decline of heavy industry since the mid-20th century. On the other hand a canal, as it is always brim-full of water, generally contributes to a rural landscape and it is often a corridor of rustic peace through many towns and suburbs today, remote from busy streets.

In these pages we see canals at Wolverhampton and Ellesmere Port at a time when commercial canal traffic was coming to an end, having been superseded by railways and lorries. The main cargoes carried by British Waterways' North West Division after the war were oil, flour and sugar from Ellesmere Port to Birmingham and the Black Country, which took two days by boat. The private carrier Thomas Clayton of Oldbury brought fuel oil from Ellesmere Port to Langley Green on the Titford branch of the Birmingham Canal Navigations (BCN) from 1924 to 1955, then in 1957 British Waterways started shipping barrels of lubricating oil from Ellesmere Port via Wolverhampton to Duckham's oil blending plant at Aldridge on the Daw

OLD HILL station was a typically humble little stop in the south Staffordshire Black Country on the former Great Western Railway from Smethwick Junction to Stourbridge Junction. When this picture was taken on 3 March 1962 trains stopped here on a half-hourly service between Birmingham Snow Hill and Stourbridge Junction and passengers changed here for the branch to Dudley. This line was also the route of semi-fast trains from Snow Hill to Worcester and Hereford. Here was a soot-stained, wooden booking office, waiting room and canopy on the up platform for Birmingham (left), the signal cabin sat on the down platform, and down passengers waited in an open-fronted, wooden shelter (extreme right). The two platforms were slightly offset as tracks diverged at this end of the station for the Dudley branch (off left) and at the far end for the Halesowen branch (off right). The large running-in board on the left reads: 'Old Hill Change here for Halesowen, Windmill End branch and Dudley'. The Halesowen branch closed to general passenger service in 1927 but the line went on beyond Halesowen to Longbridge and workmen's trains continued to use the branch to the Austin motor works there till 1958 and goods trains till 1964. The Great Western water tank stood at the up end of the down platform, handy for engines off the Halesowen branch. The Dudley branch closed to passengers in 1964 and to goods a few years later. Trains still stop at Old Hill today but the old wooden station was badly damaged by fire in 1967 and rebuilt in 1968 looking like a Portakabin dressed in pale grey brick with a felted concrete top and plastic weatherboarding above the windows and doors.

The signal cabin closed in 1973 following resignalling. Old Hill now has a half-hourly service of diesel multiple units on an extended run up through Snow Hill to Shirley or Stratford and down to Stourbridge or Worcester.

End branch, but this traffic was shortlived because British Waterways neglected to dredge the Wyre & Essington Canal. The hard winter of 1962-63, when boats were locked in the ice for 13 weeks and traffic shifted to road haulage, spelled the demise of the already uneconomic canal carrying trade and most boats never moved again.

In 1965 the new Birmingham & Midland Canal Carrying Company revived narrow boat cargoes with trips from the BCN to the Thames, Severn, Trent and Mersey. In this context the Black Country also saw a revival of canal traffic in timber from Manchester to Olton and aluminium from Walsall to Ellesmere Port, where it was trans-shipped via river barges to Liverpool. The last cargoes were carried in 1970 when the Birmingham & Midland

WOLVERHAMPTON British Waterways' narrow boats *Severn Dolphin* and *Mendip* are double-berthed on the Birmingham Canal at Broad Street bridge on 25 June 1960. Trolleybus wires turn the corner into Railway Street on the left. *Severn Dolphin* of Worcester (left) was inherited from the Severn & Canal Carrying Company on nationalisation in 1948 and was carrying coal from Brownhills to the Royal Worcester porcelain factory from 1959 to 1961. *Mendip* of Northwich (right), new to British Waterways in 1949, made two round trips a week with chocolate crumb from Cadbury's Knighton factory on the Shropshire Union Canal to Cadbury's Bournville factory on the Worcester & Birmingham Canal. These two boats display the British Waterways colour scheme of yellow and blue, which replaced the traditional 'rose and castle' decorations and drab wartime colours. Here at Broad Street, Wolverhampton, British Waterways had a depot for trans-shipment to local road haulage, a fitting shop for servicing boat engines and a washroom for crews.

and Duckham's experimented in shipping lubricating oil in tanks in narrow boats from Ellesmere Port to Aldridge. Again this proved uneconomic because of British Waterways' arrears of maintenance and the undredged accumulation of junk along the route, which slowed progress and limited the payload of boats. In the trial period, January to September 1970, the nine loaded trips lasted anything from eight days to 2½ weeks because of these obstructions! It was impossible to go on.

The 1968 Transport Act recognised the growing use of canals for pleasure cruising and teams of volunteers helped to restore hundreds of miles of disused and overgrown canals and ruined locks. In 2012 British Waterways was succeeded by the Canal & River Trust, which inherited a fleet of work boats to maintain 2,200 miles of waterways, including 100 miles of the BCN as links in the national cruiseways and 336 miles of broad canals and river navigations as commercial waterways feeding the Humber. The Trust also inherited 2,555 listed buildings including the three canal museums at Stoke Bruerne, Gloucester and Ellesmere Port.

Ellesmere Port, originally the seaward terminus of the canal from Ellesmere in Shropshire, is on the Cheshire bank of the Mersey. The river name is from the Anglo-Saxon 'Mæres-ea', the 'boundary river', part of the Humber-Mersey line marking the border between the Anglian kingdoms of Mercia and Northumbria. The Cheshire bank of the estuary from Runcorn to Birkenhead is fringed by industry, backed by wooded hills and dairy pastures producing the famous Cheshire cheese.

In the late 19th and early 20th centuries there were ten **Mersey ferries** from the Cheshire bank of the estuary to Liverpool: from Eastham, New Ferry, Rock Ferry, Tranmere, Birkenhead, Monks' Ferry, Woodside, Seacombe, Egremont and New Brighton. Woodside ferry, on the direct road from Chester to Liverpool, was the shortest and

oldest ferry passage, with a Royal charter dated 1330. Some of these ferries were already in being when they were mentioned in the earliest extant records: Woodside in 1282, Seacombe in 1330, Tranmere in 1541, Rock Ferry in 1660, and New Ferry in 1774. New Ferry, Rock Ferry and Woodside were adopted by Birkenhead Corporation, and Seacombe, Egremont and New Brighton by Wallasey Corporation. The other ferries were privately owned and the last of them, at Eastham, closed in 1929. Woodside and Seacombe had floating roads on pontoons to the landing stages for the separate vehicular ferries that for many years preceded the opening of the Mersey road tunnel in 1934. The vehicular ferries, also known as goods ferries or 'luggage boats', carried on at Woodside till 1941 and at Seacombe till 1947.

New Ferry was knocked out of service by a ship colliding with the pier in 1924, Rock Ferry service closed in 1939, and Egremont pier was also wrecked by a ship in 1941, after the ferry service had been closed in 1939 for the duration of the war – never to reopen. There was a slow decline in the number of ferry passengers from a peak in 1950-52 as the Mersey railway and road tunnels and increasing car ownership siphoned off the patronage. The night ferry from Woodside was withdrawn in 1956 and from Seacombe in 1962. The New Brighton service closed in 1971 with the decline of the seaside resort, leaving only Woodside and Seacombe ferries to Liverpool during daytime. From 1980 the two services were combined with one vessel on a one-way, triangular run between Seacombe, Woodside and Liverpool. Birkenhead and Wallasey bus routes that terminated at Woodside and Seacombe ferries were diverted through the road tunnels after bus service deregulation in 1986, drawing more passengers from the ferries. The unthinkable happened in 2010 when Woodside ferry closed; it had been running since about AD

Left: **ELLESMERE PORT** Two swans are mirrored in the still water of the middle basin of the derelict terminus of the Shropshire Union Canal in September 1962. The canal, locks and docks are silting up with mud and abandoned barges and narrow boats are slowly decaying and sinking; plant and machinery are rusting and weeds push up through the brick paving. The buildings in the picture are warehouses, workshops, stables, the gas works and the main hydraulic and pumping station. The main cargoes handled here were clay, flint, lime and bone ash for the Staffordshire potteries, grain to the granaries, cattle food and flour from the mills, iron ore for the Black Country, and ironware coming back. Other cargoes were coal, slag, oil, timber, bricks, cement, soap, sugar and general merchandise, all manhandled in sacks, barrels and bundles or by shovel and wheelbarrow. The main cargoes after the war were flour and sugar to Birmingham and oil to the Black Country, all of which ended in 1955. Today this scene has been restored as part of the National Waterways Museum, opened in 1976 and run by the Waterways Trust.

Right: **ROCK FERRY** pier and landing stage were still open for use by Mersey tugmen calling ashore for supplies, by local yachtsmen and fishermen to store their dinghies, by anglers and by promenaders for 18 years after the ferry closed. The users were charged 1d in the tollhouse at the pier entrance. The tug berthed here at the landing stage is a 'Cock' tug of the Liverpool Screw Towing & Lighterage Company. The stage retained the old ferry fog bell tower and navigation light and one of the two arched-roof passenger shelters. The lean-to extension was added during the Second World War to convert the

building for storage. The stage was 150 feet long and 45 feet wide, about the size of a Mersey ferry steamer of the period 1930-60.

Birkenhead Corporation ran a half-hourly ferry service from here to Liverpool until closure in 1939. The service extended to New Ferry until that pier

was wrecked by a ship in 1922. The Eastham ferry company's double-ended paddle steamers also called at Rock Ferry on the way between Eastham and Liverpool till that service ended in 1929; they were the last paddle steam ferries on the Mersey. The pier and landing stage closed in 1957 and were removed.

1150, endowed with a Royal Charter for the right of passage from 1330. Today there is only a morning and afternoon peak-time ferry between Seacombe and Liverpool and an off-peak river cruise calling at Seacombe, Woodside and Liverpool, which can serve as an elongated and more expensive ferry passage for passengers not going by tunnel. There are only two vessels on the entire roster and the spare one perpetuates a tradition of cruises up and down the Manchester Ship Canal.

Back in their heyday the Mersey ferries had two vessels on each service by day and one on each passage hourly through the night. They were the biggest river passenger steamers in British waters, sturdy and robust to ride the storms of the wide river estuary and large enough to carry, variously, from 1,400 to 2,200 passengers per trip. They were navigated with great skill across the busy shipping lanes by day and night, in fog and storm, with the aid of Seacombe-based radar, and the 150-foot-long steamers, with no bow thrusters, were swung round against the surge of the 6-knot tideway to berth at Liverpool landing stage with only 5 feet between them. The fresh air and close-up views of world shipping were a daily tonic for the bowler hat and briefcase brigade of businessmen, who paraded two and three abreast anti-clockwise around the promenade decks of the steamers on the three-quarter-mile passages from Woodside and Seacombe in the peak periods. On Sunday mornings Woodside ferry conveyed hundreds of cyclists on their way from Liverpool to Wirral and Wales and back again in the evening. In the summer season the 2¼-mile ferry trip downriver to New Brighton was like a sea cruise in itself for the thousands of day trippers from Liverpool heading for the sands and fairground. Wallasey Ferries also offered afternoon and evening dance cruises from Liverpool and New Brighton 11 miles out to sea to the Bar lightship and occasional cruises up the Manchester Ship Canal.

As the New Brighton ferry steamed downriver, **Wallasey** lay along the left bank from Birkenhead docks to the sea. Wallasey was originally an island at the northern tip of the Wirral peninsula, surrounded by the Irish Sea, the River Mersey, a wide creek called Wallasey Pool and tidal marshes where Bidston Moss and Leasowe are now. As the marshes silted up it became what it is today: a plateau, 190 feet high, on a peninsula between the sea, the river and the docks that were built up Wallasey Pool from Morpeth Dock in 1843 to Bidston Dock in 1933. The headwaters of the creek still lay west of Bidston Dock as a fishing lake.

The name Wallasey was Anglo-Saxon 'Wealas'ey', the 'Welshmen's island', an isolated Celtic refuge after King Æthelfrith of Northumbria split the Celtic alliance between Cumbria and Cambria (Wales) at the battle of Chester about AD 613-16 to extend Anglian settlement to the Irish Sea. Wallasey is therefore a possessive name, Wallas'ey, so it was spelled phonetically Wallizee or Wallazey on old maps and records.

The towns of Wallasey, Liscard, Poulton and Seacombe were the original villages on the island or peninsular plateau, followed centuries later by the Victorian and Edwardian towns of Egremont, New Brighton and Upper Brighton, built in the civil parish of Liscard. All are now developed into one urban area, but they retain their individual names and shopping centres. At the time of our review there were three Wallaseys: (1) the civil parish of the original village, now a town; (2) the built-up area on the peninsular plateau; and (3) the county borough extending west to Leasowe, Moreton and Saughall Massie. This is to explain the nomenclature used in the captions to the photographs; the locations are identified by the names of the individual towns rather than the blanket name of the geographical or municipal Wallasey.

I lived in the town of Wallasey from 1949 to

1952, aged 11 to 14, at the peak of the post-war revival period of industry, the docks and public transport. We then moved home to Kent, but I became so nostalgic about Merseyside that in 1954, at age 16, I returned by the Margate-Birkenhead through train (via Guildford) to spend two weeks' holiday photographing the streets, docks and ferries for my own pleasure, little thinking that they would ever be published, let alone in later years when they would be out of date! Most of those pictures appeared in my book *Merseyside: The Indian Summer* (Silver Link Publishing, 2007).

My love of old Merseyside also manifested itself

Right: **WALLASEY** The classic Wallasey bus in the typically wide, quiet, tree-lined streets of Wallasey. This is No 93, one of the 1946 stock of Metropolitan-Cammell-bodied Leyland PD1s, at its terminal lay-over in Grove Road at the junction with Hose Side Road (ahead) and Warren Drive (to the left). This was the terminus of route 6 from Seacombe ferry. Bus 93 was sold out of service in 1959 to a dealer at Walmer Bridge near Preston and exported to Sarajevo, Jugoslavia, in 1960 for further service.

Wallasey route 6 followed a devious, zigzag route through streets broad and narrow, threading through Wallasey, Liscard and Egremont to Seacombe. It went via Belvidere Road, Rullerton Road, Mill Lane, Westminster Road, Grosvenor Street, Martin's Lane, Serpentine Road, Trafalgar Road, Brighton Street and Demesne Street to the ferry, returning via Church Road instead of Demesne Street. On fine summer Saturday and Sunday afternoons from 1947 the route was extended from Grove Road via Sandcliffe Road to New Brighton seafront, then from 1950 the extension was via Harrison Drive to Wallasey Beach. With the decline in the fortunes of public transport route 6 closed in 1965.

in my ownership of an old Wallasey bus. It was easier than preserving a ferry steamer, tramcar or steam lorry. In 1973, while living at Southport, I bought one of the 1951 stock of standard Wallasey buses when it was withdrawn from service. I stabled it, in turn, at the Southport Locomotive & Transport Museum, Colne bus garage, Burscough airfield, Tranmere shipyard and finally the new Birkenhead transport museum. I restored it and drove it on excursions over its old routes for 30 years till I moved to Norfolk. It is now the only preserved survivor of 118 buses with this style of body built for Wallasey from 1937 to 1951 and is resident in the Birkenhead transport museum.

After 33 years as a newspaper reporter and feature writer at Canterbury, Kendal, Southport and at Campbeltown, where I was also photographer and editor, I 'changed horses' at age 53, returning to Cheshire to drive Chester's city and country buses (1991-99) and be near my own bus at Birkenhead, just a 15-mile cycle ride away. Nine years later, to escape Chester's traffic signals and jams, I migrated east – in the opposite direction to this travelogue – to Norfolk for another nine years' driving country buses from Holt, retiring at age 70. Bus driving was a hobby to me but the pleasure of doing it commercially was offset by impractical schedules for safety and comfort, which I suspect are a result of the 1986 deregulation.

Left: **POPPY LINE** There I was in the middle of a field, about to take a photograph of the poppies among the barley in this view between Sheringham and Weybourne, when a train emerged out of the landscape. I had no idea there was a railway nearby. The train was a two-car, green, BR Derby lightweight diesel multiple unit of 1955 on its way from Cromer to Melton Constable, the last remnant of the former Midland & Great Northern Joint Railway, in August 1961. This line closed in 1964 but was taken over by volunteers for preservation and reopened for service in 1975 as the North Norfolk Railway, running 5½ miles from Sheringham to Holt and branded 'The Poppy Line'. This north-east corner of Norfolk was called 'Poppyland' by Clement Scott, a Victorian columnist in *The Daily Telegraph*, and he made it a fashionable area to visit.

BURNHAM MARKET village green on the B1155 road from Docking to Holkham is seen first on 16 May 1962 – a placid scene with a modest BP petrol station on the left and a 1959 Austin A35 van parked on the right. At that time Burnham Market was the terminus of the ex-GER west Norfolk freight branch from Heacham, which closed in 1964.

The equivalent view on 30 August 2013 shows the rise in motorcar ownership in the second half of the 20th century. There was hardly a car to be seen in the first picture, in contrast to the second, where there is hardly a parking space to be found (the space behind the red car had just been vacated before the photograph was taken). Today North Street (left), Front Street (right) and the B1155 road through the green are overwhelmed with parked cars that disfigure this attractive village. Otherwise the scene has been enhanced by maturing trees, the cottages are unchanged or restored, and the overhead wire poles have gone (except the one on the extreme right, now without crossbars). Many of the homes around the green have been converted to estate agencies, restaurants and shops selling expensive clothes, gifts, arts and crafts as the village has become a Mecca for holiday cottages and retirement homes for wealthy people, mainly from London and the Home Counties. Most picturesque old towns and villages of England are now not worth a picture because they are spoiled by motorcars.

Cambridgeshire

CAMBRIDGE On 18 May 1958 Drummer Street bus station is in a glade of mature trees with the station offices and waiting room under a steep pitched roof on an island platform in the middle of the road. Three bus companies are represented here: the Eastern Counties Omnibus Company, of Norwich (first on the right), Premier Travel, of Cambridge (second right), and the United Counties Omnibus Company, of Northampton (left). The two 'omnibus companies' were in the Tilling/BTC group that was nationalised from 1948 and their buses were post-war Eastern-bodied Bristols, the Eastern Counties in red and cream and the United Counties in green and cream. Premier was an independent company and this second-hand, ex-Southdown wartime utility Weymann-bodied Guy is in Premier's blue and cream.

Cambridge bus station is still here with trees on the right, but occupies a smaller site. The island buildings have gone, the number of loading bays has been reduced and the buses line up side-by-side in a row to a front-loading platform on the right with an overall canopy, and have to reverse out into the path of buses entering the station. None of the bus companies represented in this photograph are to be found here today as they have all been sold to new companies.

Lincolnshire

BOSTON Railways across the flat fens of west Norfolk, north Cambridgeshire and south Lincolnshire feature little in the way of cuttings, embankments, bridges or viaducts, and most highway crossings are on the level with the railway and were paved with timber until late in the second half of the 20th century. This is Maud Foster, the crossing of the Skegness-Nottingham line and Frithville Road on the northern outskirts of Boston, on 15 June 1970, featuring a Great Northern Railway signal cabin, heavy timber crossing gates, timber paving, the Italianate GN railwayman's house, a GN semaphore signal on a latticed steel post and a row of telegraph poles carrying the railway's internal telephone lines. The timber signal cabin, mounted on a brick locking room, had a 12-lever frame controlling this and two nearby level crossings. The cabin, cottage and signal in this picture all dated from 1877.

Sections of line across Lincolnshire were singled in 1981, and this section is single from Sibsey to Hubbert's Bridge, except through Boston station. Maud Foster signal cabin was removed in 1985 as this and other crossings along the line are now protected by colour-light signals and barriers automated by mechanical treadles or electric currents triggered by approaching trains. This crossing has been repaved in asphalt with steel panels flanking the rails. The cottage was still there at the time of writing and the line was still controlled by traditional mechanical signalling and semaphore signals, but due for complete modernisation.

Left: **HUBBERT'S BRIDGE** was a quaint, wooden halt, with derelict oil lanterns, alongside the South Forty Foot Drain in Holland Fen on the line between Boston and Sleaford, also pictured here on 15 June 1970. The line and the halt are still open today for trains between Nottingham, Grantham and Skegness but the track converges from double to single immediately east of the platforms and the halt has been rebuilt with platforms paved in asphalt, a steel and glass shelter, tall electric lamp posts, and small metal nameplates. The brick goods shed on the left has gone and the stockade of old railway sleepers that fenced the former coal yard from the down platform has been replaced by a timber post-and-wire fence.

Right: **GRIMSBY** British Railways ran these large single-deck tramcars on the Grimsby & Immingham Electric Railway to carry workers to Immingham Dock, which was developed by the Great Central Railway in 1906-12. The railway was opened by the GCR to Immingham (town) in 1912 and Immingham Dock in 1913. These original GCR cars, built between 1911 and 1915, were still in service when the line closed in 1961. They were built by the Brush Electrical Engineering Company at Loughborough, 54 feet long with 72 seats. Car No 3 in front was built in 1911. With the growth of industries along the way from 1948, the service was supplemented by ex-Newcastle and ex-Gateshead single-deck bogie tramcars in 1948 and 1951 respectively. The cars ran right around the clock on a basic half-hourly service with extra cars at peak times, when a total of 19 cars were in service, including six of these big GCR cars in convoy for the change of shift at Immingham Dock.

The line was single on bullhead rail on sleepers with passing loops and a 500-volt overhead wire, and ran alongside a steam freight line on a 5-mile straight across the flat, semi-industrial fenland between the two towns. In addition, there was 1¼ miles of double street track in Grimsby and half a mile of single track on street in Immingham, where cars reversed for the 1-mile extension of 1913 on roadside reservation to the dock. The line passed to the LNER in 1923 and to BR in 1948; the former company's carriage liveries gave way to BR multiple unit green with the 'lion and wheel' emblem on the sides. Owing to the peak-time congestion of tramcars, the street section in Grimsby closed in 1956 and the Grimsby terminus was cut back to Cleveland Bridge (over the railway to Alexandra Dock), where this picture was taken on 18 July 1958. Buses replaced the closed section, but many workers obviously came here by bicycle. Fares on the remaining 6½ miles to Immingham Dock were 1 shilling single and 1s 6d return. The off-peak and night service was replaced by buses in 1959 on the zigzag 11-mile road route. The electric railway closed with the opening of a direct motor road to Immingham Dock in 1961.

IMMINGHAM Eight cars stand at Immingham Dock terminus of the Grimsby & Immingham Electric Railway on the same day. The two cars at the end of the line are ex-Gateshead Corporation bogie cars built in 1927 and sold to BR in 1951 when Gateshead tramways closed. They would take up service after the first six ex-GCR cars have cleared the dockers at the next change of shift. The GCR, Newcastle and Gateshead cars on this line were the only clerestory-roofed stock still run by BR at that time. Thanks to BR's purchase and life extension of the ex-Gateshead single-deckers, two of them from this line are now preserved at the National Tramway Museum, Crich, and at the North of England Open Air Museum, Beamish, back in County Durham.

BROCKLESBY station, on the main line from Sheffield to Grimsby and Cleethorpes, is a good example of architectural stations found on great country estates. It was built on the 50,000-acre estate of Brocklesby Hall, seat of the Earl of Yarborough, Charles Anderson-Pelham, a philanthropist, model landlord and chairman of the Great Grimsby & Sheffield Junction Railway (later the Great Central). He hoped the coming of the railway, in 1848, would improve the prosperity of his tenant farmers. The railway company had a good standard of station architecture, by Weightman and Hadfield of Sheffield, and the Earl insisted that this station was built of red brick with limestone dressings in the Jacobean style with Dutch gables and his own private waiting room. The station was 1½ miles from the hall and the village of the same name and passengers were scarce for this noble station. This picture was taken from the island platform looking west on 15 June 1970, one year after the withdrawal of station staff, and the platforms are in need of weeding. Four tracks ran through here because of the heavy freight traffic, but one track had been removed by the time of this picture. Brocklesby Junction signal cabin (right) was built by the GCR in 1914 and controlled the junction east of the station where the line divided to Grimsby and to Immingham Dock and New Holland. West of Brocklesby, beyond Barnetby, the line divided to Lincoln, Gainsborough and Scunthorpe. The station closed in 1993 and the signal cabin was decommissioned in 2015 following resignalling. Both listed buildings, the station house is now a private residence and the signal cabin is owned by Network Rail.

Left: **NEW HOLLAND PIER** This windswept wooden railway terminus on a quarter-mile-long pier on the Lincolnshire bank of the Humber was the landing place for the ferry passage to Hull from 1848 till 1981, when the suspension road bridge upriver replaced the ferry. Trains from Grimsby connected with the railway-owned ferry. The coal trucks on the centre road of this three-track layout were for coaling the ferry steamers. The coal was trans-shipped from the trucks on the pier by small, pneumatic-tyred, four-wheel 'tubs', towed by small electric tractors up and down the bridge to the landing stage and manhandled on deck to the stokehold hatch. Motorists using the ferry had to drive along the timber station platform and down the hinged bridges to the landing stage – on a gradient of 1 in 9 at low tide.

There were other ferries across the Humber from Roman times, but New Holland ferry, which began in 1803, was the sole Humber crossing by 1930. New Holland was named after a creek used by smugglers of Dutch gin. The Great Grimsby & Sheffield Junction Railway took over the ferry in 1846, then built the pier and opened the railway from Grimsby in 1848. For a few months of 1848 New Holland and Hull were on the railway route from London to Scotland via Peterborough, Grimsby, Selby and York, passengers and mails crossing the ferry, till a continuous and more direct railway link was completed further inland. The railway ferry passed in turn to the GCR, LNER and BR.

The pier is now owned by New Holland Bulk Services, exporting wheat, barley and rape seed and importing animal feed, aggregates and stone. The wooden platforms, station buildings and signal cabin are still there, but the space between the platforms is covered by conveyors and pipelines to the pier head.

Above: **NEW HOLLAND PIER** This was the way we crossed the Humber from Lincolnshire to Yorkshire on foot and by car before the suspension road bridge opened in 1981. BR still ran coal-fired paddle steamers on this passage until 1978, superseded by a diesel-electric paddler. It was a 20-minute passage from here to Hull on the Yorkshire bank, seen on the distant horizon. The PS *Tattersall Castle*, seen berthed on 16 June 1970, was built in William Gray's yard at West Hartlepool in 1934 for the LNER, like her sister ship on this passage, *Wingfield Castle*. These side-loading car ferries replaced older vessels that had to load and unload vehicles by crane. The passenger accommodation was forward of the bridge and the vehicle deck was aft. The third vessel on this passage was the identical PS *Lincoln Castle*, built by A. & J. Inglis at Glasgow in 1941. Two were in service while one was kept spare. In 1948 the *Tattersall Castle* was the first paddle steamer in the world to be equipped with radar, to cope with Humber fogs. She retired from service in 1973 and *Wingfield Castle* in 1974, when BR drafted its 1947 diesel-electric ferry *Farringford* from the Solent to maintain the two-ship service. Humber ferries were always paddlers because of the shallow draughts required for this wide river with its many sandbanks. The *Lincoln Castle* was the last coal-fired paddle steamer in British waters when it retired from service in 1978, leaving the *Farringford* to soldier on alone till the ferry closed in 1981. The *Tattersall Castle*, much altered, is berthed as a floating restaurant at Victoria Embankment, Westminster.

HUMBER FERRY We are now crossing the Humber on the foredeck of the 1934 *Wingfield Castle* from New Holland to Hull on the same day. The radar scanner can be seen on the extreme right. The wind was singing in the rigging and the paddle wheels threshed the water with a regular rhythm while the heartbeat of the pistons could be felt underfoot. Sister ship *Tattersall Castle* is passing on the left on passage to New Holland.

WATFORD GAP Part of a line-up of Standerwick and Scout 'Gay Hostess' double-deck coaches is seen at Watford Gap service station on motorway express service from London to north-west England on 12 September 1965. This was the first year of the integrated motorway express services operated by Ribble Motor Services of Preston through its two subsidiary express coach companies, W. C. Standerwick of Blackpool and Scout Motor Services of Preston, which had been taken over by Ribble in 1932 and 1961 respectively and still operated under their separate names. These are all Metropolitan-Cammell-bodied Leyland Atlanteans of 1960-61, fitted out by Weymann with luxury seating, serveries and toilets. There were 34 seats upstairs and 16 downstairs, and smartly dressed hostesses served food and drinks. The first four coaches in the line are destined for Colne, Blackburn, Blackpool and Blackpool; others in the line were going to Skipton, Preston and Keswick.

LEICESTER Lorries on the A6 trunk road through the city mix with local traffic and tramcars in this photograph taken outside the railway station (right) on London Road in 1948. Passengers stand on the steps of the conductor's platform, ready to alight, as inbound tramcar 135 on route 1, Belgrave to Western Park, approaches the stop for the station, followed by a 1947 Vauxhall car. An oncoming tramcar is climbing the slope from Granby Street. London Road station was rebuilt by the Midland Railway in 1892 with this long, west-facing, arcaded portico in orange-brown terracotta with separate levels and arches for arrivals and departures by cab. At this time Leicester had four railway stations – Belgrave Road, Central, London Road and West Bridge – but this is now the city's only one.

The portico and booking hall survive as listed buildings but the platforms were completely rebuilt in the 1970s and '80s. The new inner ring road now passes through this location with a three-way junction in front of the station, and the handsome buildings beyond the station have been demolished. The white buildings on the corner of Granby Street in the background still stand but two incongruous skyscrapers, one in profiled concrete, the other with blue panels, now form the backdrop to this view. *George Greenwood*

WARWICK Church Street leads from the central crossroads to St Mary's parish church with its 174-foot tower; the arch under the tower leads into Northgate Street. On 6 July 1958 a Midland bus stops on its way to Leamington. The Birmingham & Midland Motor Omnibus Company (BMMO) designed and built most of its own buses in its central workshops at Edgbaston from 1924 to 1970. Its post-war single-deckers were of the underfloor-engine design with full-width fronts and front entrances, like this 1950 model S10 with a BMMO chassis and engine and an 8-foot-wide, 44-seat Brush body to BMMO design. The buses, painted overall red, carried the fleet name 'Midland' on the side panels and the company was branded 'Midland Red' on stop flags, timetables and publicity. The company operated more than 1,000 local and limited-stop services from 28 depots throughout Warwickshire, Leicestershire, Worcestershire, Herefordshire, Shropshire and south Staffordshire as well as parts of neighbouring counties.

BIRMINGHAM Three Corporation buses in dark blue and cream emerge from Colmore Row to join Congreve Street in Victoria Square on 16 May 1959, with the Council House (right) and the Town Hall (left) as a noble backdrop. These were Birmingham's distinctive standard buses of the period with identical bodies by Crossley, Metropolitan-Cammell and Saunders Roe on Crossley, Daimler and Guy chassis; they were in service from 1950 to 1977. Bus stop flags in Birmingham were circular, both for the Corporation and the Midland, the latter having a 'circle and bar' sign based on a bus wheel and tyre with the company name across the bar. Two Midland buses can just be seen in Congreve Street loading outside the Art Gallery, marked by the 160-foot clock tower known as 'Big Brum'.

The Council House, built in 1874-79, housed the city council chamber, committee rooms and offices. The grand, classical Town Hall with its Corinthian colonnades on a massive, rock-faced, arcaded base was built in 1832-37 for public assemblies and concerts. The architect was Joseph Hansom, who invented the Patent Safety Cab, the revolutionary, two-wheel, two-passenger 'Hansom cab', in 1834. This was held to be more stable than other horse-drawn carriages because of its fine balance with the axle below the passenger seat and the driver standing behind and above. By 1896 there were 7,586 Hansom cabs in London alone; they were the Victorian forerunners of the motor taxicab. The tall Victorian Gothic building behind the Town Hall is the Liberal Club of 1885, demolished in 1965 to be replaced by an incongruously modern extension of the central library, built in 1973.

The whole of this scene is now a pedestrian zone and Congreve Street, which brought the main road from Dudley into the city, has been wiped off the map and blocked by grey, grim, concrete extensions of the library and the municipal buildings.

WEDNESBURY Buses from West Bromwich (right) and Walsall (yonder) meet at this strategic junction of the Black Country, the White Horse, on 7 July 1958. Here the A41 trunk road from London to Birkenhead, which is also the main road from Birmingham to Wolverhampton, forks left from Bridge Street into Holyhead Road, and Lower High Street forks right into Wednesbury town centre. The West Bromwich Corporation bus is a 1951 Weymann-bodied Daimler in two-tone blue and cream. This was the terminus of route 75 from Birmingham through West Bromwich, run jointly with Birmingham Corporation; it was formerly operated solely by Birmingham trams with the same route number. Beyond is the connecting Walsall Corporation bus in overall blue. At one time this three-way junction was the terminal meeting place of tramways from Birmingham, Walsall and Bilston and a triangular junction was laid to link the three lines. South Staffordshire Tramways' pioneer electric line from Bloxwich via Walsall terminated here in 1893 and the company later operated a 'Black Country Through Car' from Bilston to Birmingham via White Horse junction from 1912 to 1924. Then the three lines were cut back here to terminal stubs and from 1930 to 1939 Birmingham's were the only trams operated from the White Horse.

The White Horse Hotel (the white building seen over the roof of the West Bromwich bus), which gave its name to this junction, was demolished in the 1990s and the entire scene is unrecognisable today because of 'improvements' to the A41. St John's Church, built in 1846, was demolished in 1985. Left of it, Lloyd's Bank, near the apex of the junction, was demolished and rebuilt soon after this photograph was taken, but even the new bank has now closed. In the left foreground is a nice example of a blue police-public telephone post, but that has gone too.

Left: **WOLVERHAMPTON LOW LEVEL** The classical Italianate façade of the former GWR station is seen on 25 June 1960, with a Wolverhampton Corporation bus parked on the forecourt. The station was built in 1854-55 and was a main stage on the routes from Paddington to Birkenhead and Aberystwyth. It closed to passengers in 1970 together with Birmingham Snow Hill two years after Paddington-Shrewsbury trains were diverted via Birmingham New Street and Wolverhampton High Level. Low Level station was retained as a railway parcels depot until that closed in 1981.

The listed main building seen here on the down side was bought by Wolverhampton Corporation and renovated with the intention of using it as a transport museum. However, this project foundered as the building was transferred to the Black Country Development Corporation, which did nothing with it during its term of office. By the time the latter was dissolved, Wolverhampton Corporation no longer had the funds to develop a transport museum. The building, with its magnificent, classical entrance hall, is now Wolverhampton Grand Station, an events centre for banquets, conferences and weddings. The rest of the station has been demolished and redeveloped with blocks of flats and a hotel.

Right: **WOLVERHAMPTON LOW LEVEL** was the most northerly on the original Great Western broad gauge. The first GWR standard-gauge train ran from Paddington to Birkenhead in 1861, and Wolverhampton Low Level remained the relay point to change engines. Viewed from the leading coach of a Birkenhead train at the north-west end of the station on 8 May 1960, No 4903 *Aston Hall* (right) is moving forward to take over from No 6000 *King George V* at the head of the train and take it on to Chester; a big 'King' had to hand over to a 'Castle' or a 'Hall' because of the limited axle load on bridges beyond Wolverhampton, and the 'Kings' were stabled here. A pannier tank engine stands in the shadow of Wednesfield Road bridge as a Wolverhampton Corporation bus crosses overhead. Although this picture was taken 12 years into the British Railways era, all three locomotives are of GWR pedigree, as are the water column, semaphore signals and signal cabin seen through the left portal of the bridge.

WOLVERHAMPTON HIGH LEVEL The handsome, Italianate façade is viewed from Railway Drive on 25 June 1960 with its Romanesque arcading and windows and the arms of the Shrewsbury & Birmingham Railway in the pediment. The SBR withdrew its alliance with the LNWR before opening and teamed up with the GWR at the adjacent Low Level station. High Level was opened by the LNWR in 1852 on the route from Birmingham New Street to Stafford. In this picture, taken in the days of BR Midland Region, a billboard advertises cheap Sunday trips to Manchester for 11s 8d return and a sign on the canopy valance directs passengers to the left through a subway to the parallel Low Level station, although it had its own road approach from Corn Hill. In the 1950s there were six lines radiating from Wolverhampton; now there are only three. During the electrification of the main line in 1964-67 BR demolished and rebuilt this station to make it look modern but, in that philistine decade, it resulted in the mean, austere, cubic composition of prefabricated concrete panels and windowless, pale grey brick walls that we have today. Its stark ugliness is ineffectively screened by a small grove of trees. Network Rail has earmarked this station to be rebuilt in the near future.

CHURCH STRETTON railway station, at 613 feet, is the highest point on the main line from Hereford to Shrewsbury. It was characteristic of Great Western main-line stations with its spacious platforms, wide canopies, ample architectural buildings, covered wooden footbridge, gas lamps, rock gardens and (though not seen in this view) large, legible station nameboards with white cast-iron capital letters on black boards in white frames on the platform ends where the trains run in. The station was relocated and rebuilt here in 1914, and its opening stimulated the town to develop as a small, secluded inland resort with hotels, shops and villas on the foothills of the Long Mynd in this beautiful valley where a Roman road passed between two great ranges of wooded hills. In this picture we are looking south along the line towards Craven Arms and Ludlow in June 1960. The station became an unstaffed halt in 1967 and the buildings were demolished and replaced by two stone shelters with sawtooth valances on the canopies and an open footbridge.

IRONBRIDGE This general view of the town on 19 June 1960 shows part of Iron Bridge & Broseley railway station in the foreground, with the level crossing, footbridge and station office, on the Severn Valley line of the former GWR from Worcester to Shrewsbury. Beyond the station the road crosses the famous iron bridge, built in 1779, over the River Severn. This was the first iron bridge in the world, and gave its name to the town; it closed to motor traffic in 1934. Over the bridge is the town centre with the arcaded Market House of 1763 in the Market Place (centre) and St Michael's parish church on the hillside. The railway closed in 1963 and the track north of Bridgnorth was dismantled, but the line south of Bridgnorth to Bewdley and Kidderminster was reopened progressively from 1970 to 1984 for preservation by the Severn Valley Railway. Iron Bridge & Broseley station nameboard is now on display in the ironworks museum at Coalbrookdale, where the iron bridge was built. This district was a cradle of the Industrial Revolution based on coal and iron found in these hills. At the time of this photograph Ironbridge was a quaint, sleepy, run-down industrial town, with fishermen in coracles on the river, before the area was promoted for tourism in the late 20th century with five museums of industrial archaeology on a heritage trail centred on the town.

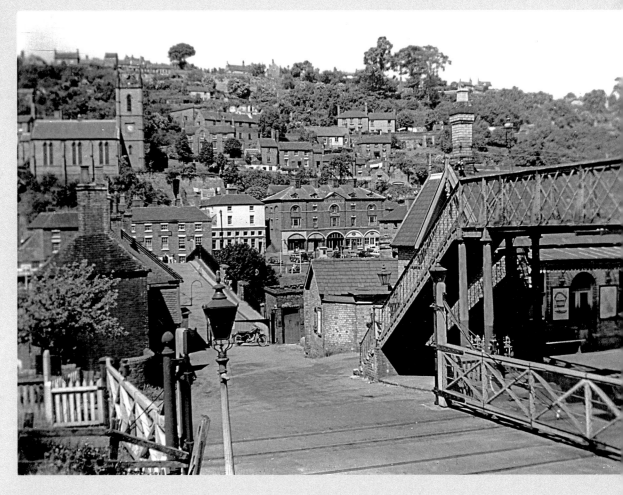

NOTTINGHAM

MIDLAND station frontage on Carrington Street was photographed on 20 March 1960. The Midland Railway rebuilt the station in 1900-04 with this west-facing Edwardian baroque portico and clock tower in orange-brown terracotta trimmed with red sandstone on the crest of the road bridge spanning the railway tracks. The bridge was rebuilt and widened at the same time. Like Leicester London Road station, the long façade is a screen with Romanesque arches giving access to a covered forecourt for cabs and carriages under a glass roof. The grand booking hall behind has yellow ochre sandstone walls with pilasters, Romanesque arches and portholes on a dado of dark green glazed tiles and is lit by a barrelled skylight. Electric overhead wires indicate that this was a city of trolleybuses with a line branching down Station Street (left). Nottingham's large trolleybus network closed in 1965-66. A green Corporation AEC motorbus rolls by towards the city centre.

Derbyshire

DERWENT VALLEY This landscape view between Grindleford and Hathersage on 17 July 1958 illustrates how the railway blends with and enhances the countryside and gives the landscape a focal point of interest. The white plume of steam in the middle distance marks a westbound freight train as steam traction still ruled this former Midland Railway route between Sheffield and Manchester, with goods trains running all night. The other railway route between Sheffield and Manchester was the former Great Central line via Woodhead, which was electrified in 1954 but closed in 1981, leaving only this line linking the two great industrial areas. This is known as the Hope Valley line from the high point of the route through Hope and Edale in the High Peak district further west. This is one of the most scenic railway routes in Britain, theatrically revealed as the trains emerge from the long tunnels (from Dore to Grindleford and from Chinley to Edale) at each end of this passage through the heathery moors, craggy escarpments and well-wooded dales.

Cheshire

ALTRINCHAM & BOWDON

These 1931-vintage, 1,500-volt DC electric multiple unit trains were still groaning along the 8-mile line from Manchester Oxford Road through Stretford to the more salubrious Cheshire suburbs of Sale and Altrincham south of the Mersey when this picture was taken at the Altrincham terminus on 9 April 1969. Meanwhile work was commencing on the half-mile between London Road South Junction and Oxford Road to re-electrify the whole line to 25,000 volts AC.

This all-compartment stock was built by the Metropolitan-Cammell Carriage & Wagon Company, Birmingham, for a joint venture by the LNER and the LMSR to operate the first railway in Britain to be electrified at 1,500 volts DC, being the suburban section of the former Cheshire Lines Committee route from Manchester to Northwich and Chester. The CLC was a joint committee of the Great Northern, Midland and Great Central railways, thus from 1923 it was still a joint operation of the LNER and LMSR. The line's high-voltage AC era did not last long as the section reverted to a 750-volt DC light railway in 1992, the first leg of Manchester's new tramway system.

CHESTER One of Chester City Transport's seven new Massey-bodied Guy buses of 1961-62 stops in Eastgate Street in the evening sunlight and shadows of 16 August 1962 on route 5 to Saltney. These were Chester's first 8-foot-wide buses, 30 feet long with forward entrances. The bonnet and radiator was designed for a South African order and was known in Britain as the 'Johannesburg front'. Guys dominated the Corporation bus fleet after the war and Chester had the last Guy bus built for Britain, in 1969.

Eastgate Street was the main thoroughfare of the city before the inner ring road was built; it is now totally pedestrianised. Behind the bus is the large Grosvenor Hotel and the Georgian stone arch over the street with its Victorian clock turret, marking the site of the former fortified East Gate of the city. Georgian archways now carry the continuous circuit of city walls over the main streets north, south, east and west. On the right is one of the 'rows' of two-tiered shops with the first-floor row behind a covered walkway, integrated into the building, above the ground-floor shops, a feature found only on the main streets of this old city centre.

Below: **CHESTER GENERAL** Steam in the evening sunshine at the west end of the station on 11 August 1962, with locomotives left, right and centre and a group of trainspotters on the end of the platform. A GWR 'Manor' Class 4-6-0 idles in the bay platform (left), and an LMSR Fowler 4MT tank engine has two vans in tow in the shadow of Hoole Road bridge. Chester No 5 signal cabin stands beyond the bridge and in the background is the profile of a locomotive on the turntable within the triangle of tracks between Chester station and those left to Shrewsbury and Holyhead and right to Birkenhead.

Right: **ELLESMERE PORT** station is seen looking east along the Hooton-Helsby line to the Mersey Iron Works (right), Burnell's steel mills (left), Stanlow oil refinery, Ince power station and the hills of the Delamere Forest. This line was part of the GWR and LNWR joint line from Birkenhead Docks to Manchester, opened in 1863, and this station was one of the original Jacobean-style buildings in red sandstone with curved Dutch gables and clusters of tall chimneys in red

pressed Ruabon brick. Ellesmere Port No 3 signal cabin sits on the west end of the eastbound platform. The photograph was taken in September 1962 from the road bridge opened in 1961 to replace the busy town centre level crossing on the main street.

When the station opened in 1863 it was named Whitby Locks after the nearest village and the terminal locks on the railway-owned Shropshire Union Canal – before the town of Ellesmere Port was built. Burnell's steel works shut down in 1962 and the Mersey Iron Works, founded by the Wolverhampton Corrugated Iron Company, carried on till closure in 1997. The latter company migrated had here in 1903, building houses for the workers and creating the suburb of Wolverham; it was the town's biggest single employer with 1,850 workers in 1939. The two iron and steel works together once employed 2,600 people.

Left: **ELLESMERE PORT** Manchester Ship Canal railway tank engines stand outside the engine shed and workshop at West Junction on the Helsby-Hooton main line in September 1962. This repair shop serviced the seven MSC locomotives that worked a 20-mile network of industrial railways east and west of the town, using the BR main line in between. West Junction served the docks, ship canal wharves, the large cattle food and flour mills seen on the skyline, and North Road industrial estate, including Bowaters' pulp and paper mills and two oil companies. East Junction served the oil refineries and ship canal wharves at Stanlow. The ship canal railways at Ellesmere Port were isolated from the rest of the MSC railways, which ran alongside the canal from Manchester to Warrington, but the entire system has since closed together with the decline of industry and shipping and the growth of road haulage. The dockside granaries and mills in the background of this picture have all been demolished.

Right and below: **ELLESMERE PORT** Here the Shropshire Union Canal locked down to the trans-shipment docks connecting with the River Mersey and, from 1894, the Manchester Ship Canal, cut along the south bank of the river estuary. In this picture, taken in September 1962, are two flights of locks, dating from 1795: broad locks in the centre for barges and narrow locks on the right for narrow boats being lowered and lifted between the upper and middle basins. The lock between the warehouses

in the background took boats to the lower level, where goods were exchanged with Mersey barges and seagoing ships, either directly or by storage in the warehouses. The port facilities were much enlarged and aggrandised by the civil engineer Thomas Telford in 1830-44 with a large new trans-shipment dock on the middle level and a complex of massive stone warehouses serving both lower and middle levels. Some Black Country narrow boats ventured into the ship canal to berth at Stanlow oil refinery and they were the last regular cargo-carriers to use the Shropshire Union Canal, in 1955. The smokestack marks a hydraulic station that powered capstans, hoists and cranes and pumped water into the middle basin when it ran short.

Today all the giant trans-shipment warehouses of Telford's grand terminus have gone and the wharves of the middle and lower basins have been redeveloped with a hotel, flats and shops in a mock industrial style of architecture, as seen in the comparison view taken on 23 September 2003.

Right: **ROCK FERRY** This old ferry landing place on the Cheshire bank of the Mersey gives its name to a southern suburb of Birkenhead. The ferry passage from The Rock, in the parish of Bebington, to Liverpool dated from 1660. The red sandstone slipway (left) with its runway for horse waggons was built in 1820 and steam ferries plied from here from 1832. King George III stayed at the original Rock Hotel while hunting in Wirral, hence the Royal Rock Ferry Steam Packet Company was formed in 1836 to operate the ferry, to build a river wall and to develop the neighbourhood. The ferry service was acquired in 1896 by Birkenhead Corporation, which built the iron pier in 1899; it was 260 yards long with a suspended bridge down to the floating landing stage, from which this picture was taken in 1952. The slipway had to be shortened to accommodate the stage. The ferry service closed in 1939 but the pier remained open for tugmen, fishermen, yachtsmen and promenaders till 1957. It was then replaced by the south pier of Tranmere oil terminal in 1960. Ashore we see the Royal Rock Hotel, rebuilt in 1836, the single-storey Doric-style bath house for sailors, converted in 1896 to cottages, and the trees of Rock Park, a bosky residential estate of Italianate villas built in 1836-50 for Liverpool merchants and 'professional gentlemen' attracted here to rural Wirral by the introduction of steam ferries.

In the 1970s the hotel and Doric cottages were demolished and the cottages replaced by a block of flats; the river front is now a scene of utter dereliction, but the Royal Mersey Yacht Club and the Tranmere Sailing Club still have their headquarters here and use the slipway to row out to their yachts moored in the river.

Below right: **ROCK FERRY** station was on the GWR/LNWR main line from Chester to Birkenhead and these three tracks were the bay terminus of the Mersey Railway from Liverpool Central Low Level. The Mersey Railway was the first steam railway in Britain to be electrified, in 1903, and this was one of the original electric trains, pictured at Rock Ferry in 1954; they survived in service till 1956. The line from Liverpool ran in tunnel under the Mersey and Birkenhead, surfacing at Tranmere. It opened in 1886 with condensing steam locomotives, but the smoke in the 4 miles of tunnel with 1 in 27 and 1 in 30 gradients forced electrification. The American firm of British Westinghouse Electric did the job in 1901-03 with no interruption to the steam service! There was a power station in Birkenhead feeding 650 volts DC through a side conductor rail, the

centre rail returning current to the power station. The head office, car sheds and workshops were at Birkenhead Central station. This original stock was built by G. F. Milnes, at Hadley, Shropshire, on Baldwin-Westinghouse Electric bogies in 1900-02. A branch ran to Birkenhead Park, where it met the Wirral Railway, and when the LMSR electrified the Wirral lines in 1938 with new metal stock, these wooden trains also ran from Liverpool through to New Brighton, Monday to Saturday, and to West Kirby on Sunday, but no new LMSR stock came to Rock Ferry. The Mersey Railway, however, remained independent till nationalisation in 1948, and its dark Indian red trains were repainted in 1950-54 to BR multiple unit green. The power station closed in 1959, when the railway switched to the national grid. Rock Ferry station had six platforms, four on the four-track main line and two on the Mersey Railway, spanned by a covered wooden footbridge with four wooden lift towers. The Liverpool-Rock Ferry electrification was extended under the name Merseyrail to Hooton in 1985, Chester in 1993 and Ellesmere Port in 1994 with new BR stock. Rock Ferry station has been reduced to two platforms, with open footbridge and ramps, on the double-track through electric line; there are no main-line services and no freights to or from the docks.

Right: **BIRKENHEAD** A ship in dry dock (left) lies alongside Birkenhead Woodside railway station (right) in this photograph from August 1954. There was a row of six Grayson, Rollo & Clover Graving Docks along the Mersey bank south of Woodside station. When a ship was afloat on entering or leaving the nearest dock, its hull and superstructure towered high above trains entering and leaving the station. The ornate iron canopy covered the luggage and parcels loading bay on the south side of the station. The line-up of railway-owned vehicles drawn up under the canopy for loading comprise an Austin lorry, a Dennis van, two Karrier vans and another Austin lorry, all built in the 1940s. The clock tower of Birkenhead Town Hall dominates the skyline.

Left: **BIRKENHEAD WOODSIDE** A Paddington train is drawn up in Platform 1 inside the northernmost passenger terminus of the legendary Great Western empire in May 1959. Paddington-Birkenhead through trains ran via Banbury, Birmingham, Shrewsbury and Chester from 1861 till 1967. The Chester-Birkenhead line terminated at Grange Lane in 1840 and was extended to Monks Ferry in 1842 and diverted to Woodside in 1878. The twin-arched trainshed spanned five platforms and a motor road for parcels and luggage vans between Platforms 1 and 2. The clock tower of Birkenhead Town Hall is framed in the fan screen of the arch in the centre of this picture. Trains also ran from here along the GWR route to Pwllheli and on joint services with the Southern Railway/Region via Birmingham to Bournemouth and Margate. The GWR/BR(W) shared this terminus with the LNWR/LMSR/BR(M) for stopping passenger services on the joint lines to Chester, Helsby and West Kirby via Hooton. The West Kirby service closed in 1956, that to Margate in 1959 and to Bournemouth in 1961. Woodside station closed in 1967 and the remaining local services terminated at Rock Ferry to connect with the Mersey Railway. The listed station building was demolished and replaced by office blocks and bus and car parks. Nikolaus Pevsner's architectural guide to Cheshire described Woodside station as 'one of the few really good main line termini outside London'.

Right and below: **BIRKENHEAD WOODSIDE** The railway and bus terminus at Woodside ferry was the focal point of Birkenhead and faced Liverpool waterfront across the half-mile-wide River Mersey. A ferry has plied from Woodside on the road from Chester to Liverpool since about AD 1150. Stage coaches from Chester terminated here from 1762 and the GWR to Birkenhead (1840) was extended here in 1878. Woodside was a hamlet around the original ferry landing on the birch-wooded headland before the new town of Birkenhead was developed from a nucleus by the priory with the advent of steam ferries in 1820. Beside the trainshed in the first view (right), from August 1954, the green country buses of Crosville Motor Services, Chester, stand on the slope of Chester Street loading for Loggerheads, Chester and Heswall, while another leaves for Ellesmere Port. The first two buses are Eastern-bodied Bristol Ks, a 1948 low-bridge and a later model high-bridge. Crosville buses served Cheshire and north and mid-Wales. Down on the ferry approach are Birkenhead Corporation's blue buses. On the left is the Mersey Motor Works on the corner of Bridge Street and the black, gabled lairage of the Mersey Cattle Wharf, which imported Irish cattle. The long

pedestrian crossing has no refuge island; these 'zebra' crossings were introduced nationally in 1954 after area trials from 1949.

The busy bus station is seen again on 10 August 1961. The single-decker on the right is a 1948 Bristol L6A for Meols. The Lodekkas behind, bound for Burton, Heswall and Ellesmere Port, were new in 1960. The twin-arched trainshed (right) was the northern terminus of the Great Western Railway from 1878 till 1967.

This scene has changed completely. The railway terminus has been replaced by two red-brick office blocks, the motor works site is a car park and the lairage site is a 'business park'. The Liverpool waterfront buildings are now dwarfed by a new skyline of black, white and khaki skyscrapers of concrete and glass.

Right: **BIRKENHEAD WOODSIDE**
Stranger in town: Ribble Motor Services of Preston, which ran local and express services in Lancashire, Westmorland and Cumberland, also operated these double-deck, 50-seat, Leyland Atlantean coaches on the X25 service between Liverpool and Bristol, calling at Chester, Whitchurch, Bridgnorth, Cheltenham and Gloucester on the way. They ran through the Mersey Tunnel between Birkenhead and Liverpool. The Metropolitan-Cammell coachwork was fitted out by Weymann with reclining seats, a toilet and a servery for refreshments. The bus is pictured on Chester Street by Woodside station on 10 August 1961.

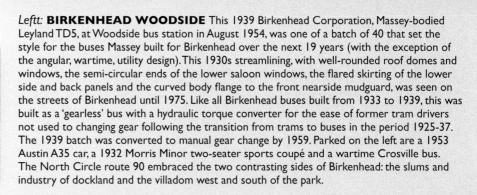

Leftt: **BIRKENHEAD WOODSIDE** This 1939 Birkenhead Corporation, Massey-bodied Leyland TD5, at Woodside bus station in August 1954, was one of a batch of 40 that set the style for the buses Massey built for Birkenhead over the next 19 years (with the exception of the angular, wartime, utility design). This 1930s streamlining, with well-rounded roof domes and windows, the semi-circular ends of the lower saloon windows, the flared skirting of the lower side and back panels and the curved body flange to the front nearside mudguard, was seen on the streets of Birkenhead until 1975. Like all Birkenhead buses built from 1933 to 1939, this was built as a 'gearless' bus with a hydraulic torque converter for the ease of former tram drivers not used to changing gear following the transition from trams to buses in the period 1925-37. The 1939 batch was converted to manual gear change by 1959. Parked on the left are a 1953 Austin A35 car, a 1932 Morris Minor two-seater sports coupé and a wartime Crosville bus. The North Circle route 90 embraced the two contrasting sides of Birkenhead: the slums and industry of dockland and the villadom west and south of the park.

Right: **BIRKENHEAD WOODSIDE** The rounded and flared body style with stout window pillars inherited from the pre-war designs can be seen on this 1949 Massey-bodied, Gardner-engined Guy bus at Woodside in August 1954. Like all Birkenhead buses of the period it had blue leather seats, chrome handrails and Art Deco lampshades. Under the bonnet was a six-cylinder Gardner diesel engine with a deep-throated throb and gear whine. This was one of a batch of 15 Guy Arabs that served Birkenhead from 1949 to 1963. A total of 85 Daimlers and Guys with this style of bodywork (including 15 rebodied wartime Guys) operated in Birkenhead in the 1950s and '60s, the last nine, built in 1956, retiring from service in 1972. This bus, No 147, is pictured alongside Woodside railway station for the New Chester Road service to Bromborough (6 miles for 5d then). Birkenhead Corporation bus routes extended well beyond the borough boundary and the blue and cream livery was seen as far afield at Eastham, Clatterbridge, Heswall, Thurstaston, Moreton and New Brighton. A Wolseley 450, also of 1949, is facing us in the single-file car park (left) through the middle of the bus station for ferry commuters.

Left: **BIRKENHEAD WOODSIDE** One of the 15 Massey-bodied Daimlers of 1950 for Birkenhead Corporation is pictured on the corner of Hamilton Street and Shore Road (left) at Woodside. It has just arrived on route 73 from Irby via Arrowe Park on 10 August 1961. These buses were in service till 1964. Birkenhead Corporation continued ordering new front-engine, rear-platform Guys and Leylands with half-width cabs and open radiators until they were no longer available. The last traditional Leyland PD2 batches in 1967 overlapped Birkenhead's first orders for rear-engine, front-entrance Daimler Fleetlines in 1964 and was followed by Leyland Atlanteans in 1968. Parked right of the bus is a 1948 Austin car of a design introduced in 1939.

Right: **BIRKENHEAD WOODSIDE** From the foot of the floating road that was used for the vehicular ferry service from 1868 to 1941 we see the twin-screw passenger ferry steamer *Bidston* arriving at the floating landing stage on the ebb tide in 1954. This steamer was built by Cammell Laird at Lower Tranmere in 1933. On the right are the barrel-roofed bridge and wooden waiting shed and the tower housing the navigation light and fog bell. We can also see Liverpool Cathedral in the background, a mile and a half away across the river. The stage dated from 1861 and the covered accommodation from 1863. It was said to be the oldest floating structure in the world when it was towed away in 1985 and replaced by the present Woodside stage.

Left: **BIRKENHEAD WOODSIDE** The ferry steamer *Hinderton* arrives on the flood tide at Woodside landing stage in 1950 on the three-quarter-mile passage from Liverpool. Through the smoky haze of industry and shipping we can see a cargo ship in mid-river and the massive granaries at Coburg Dock, Liverpool (left). *Hinderton*, 484 gross tons, was built in 1925 and set the standard design for Birkenhead Corporation ferries in service for the next 35 years, being the prototype for her three consorts, *Thurstaston, Claughton* and *Bidston*, each 487 gross tons, which followed in 1930-33. They were all twin-screw steamers built by Cammell, Laird & Company at Lower Tranmere, each 158 feet long, 43 feet in beam, licensed to carry 1,433 passengers, and coal-fired to the end. Birkenhead Corporation always gave its ferry steamers local place names, Hinderton being the old name for Lower Tranmere. Two steamers plied the passage every 10 minutes in the peak periods and every 15 minutes in the off-peak, and one steamer plied hourly through the night until the night service ended in 1956. *Hinderton* also plied excursions upriver to Eastham and downriver to the Bar lightship in 1942-48 and was occasionally on charter to Wallasey Corporation as a relief ferry on Seacombe and New Brighton services. She was retired from service in 1956 after two mid-river collisions weakened her hull plates, and was scrapped in 1958. Woodside ferry was municipalised from 1848 and traffic peaked in 1919-41 and again in 1948-50 with between 10 and 14 million passengers a year. From 1950 passengers slowly drifted to the railway and road tunnels.

BIRKENHEAD The last Birkenhead steam ferry on the Mersey was the TSS *Claughton*, built in 1930 and pictured here on passage from Woodside to Liverpool with her birthplace, Cammell Laird's shipyards at Lower Tranmere, in the background on 9 June 1961. *Claughton* retired from service at the end of that year after plying the passage for 31 years, and was scrapped in 1962. The evening sunlight picks out the pale green hull of the Shell tanker *Sepia* (42,000 tons gross) in the fitting-out basin at Laird's shipyard, which employed more than 10,000 men when it was busy. The *Sepia* was in service till 1983. Oil tankers were taking over from colliers about this time and in the left background we can see Tranmere oil terminal, which opened in 1960. Oil was piped to storage tanks onshore, thence to Stanlow refinery near Ellesmere Port.

BIRKENHEAD Corporation's first diesel ferry, the TSMV *Mountwood*, of 1960, is in a storm light on the Mersey under a grim cloud over Birkenhead and its shipyards on 26 September 1964. This vessel was not built in those shipyards of her ancestors but by Philip & Son at Dartmouth, with Crossley diesel engines, and she was slightly smaller than the steamers at 152 feet by 40 feet, 464 gross tons, and licensed for 1,200 passengers. For the first time there was a saloon on the upper foredeck, restricting the business commuters' traditional counter-clockwise, four-abreast march around the open promenade deck enjoyed on the steamers. Following the merger with Wallasey Ferries under the new Merseyside Passenger Transport Authority and the Mersey Ferries flag in 1969 and a refit in 1990 for cruising, including a fully covered bridge, this vessel has been in Mersey ferry service longer than any other and is still on the roster today, renamed *Royal Iris of the Mersey* after one of the famous old Wallasey steamers, *Royal Iris* (1906-31).

Right: **BIRKENHEAD**
This stern view of *Mountwood*'s twin sister, *Woodchurch*, shows her screws churning the water as she swings out from Liverpool landing stage on a flood tide and heads for Woodside on 14 June 1964. In the background is the silhouette of Birkenhead dockland (left) and Wallasey Town Hall (right) on the Cheshire bank. *Woodchurch* was also built in 1960, following *Mountwood* off the stocks and into service. She was laid up for sale in Morpeth Dock, Birkenhead, from 1981 to 1983, but then overhauled for further ferry service. After a major refit in 1989, again with a fully covered bridge, *Woodchurch* is also still in ferry and cruise service, now renamed *Snowdrop* after another old Wallasey ferry. A third and similar diesel ferry, *Overchurch*, from Cammell Laird in 1962, later refitted

and renamed after another old Wallasey steamer *Royal Daffodil*, was laid up in 2013 and languishes in dock. The decline in the number of passengers accelerated from 1986 with a new bus service through the Mersey Tunnel. Seacombe ferry now runs at peak times only and since 2010 there has been no Woodside ferry service as such – just an off-peak river cruise on a triangular run that calls at Woodside, Liverpool and Seacombe. The two remaining ships also carry on an old Wallasey ferries tradition of cruises up and down the Manchester Ship Canal.

Right: **BIRKENHEAD** The Great Western's farthest north railhead was Morpeth Dock goods station and sidings, where 4-6-0 locomotive No 6569 *Peatling Hall*, from Old Oak Common shed in west London, is pictured raising steam for its return trip with the evening fast freight, 'The General', to Paddington on 15 August 1962. There were numerous named fast freights and unnamed slow freights between Morpeth Dock and points on the GWR system in the Midlands, London and south Wales. The GWR aspired to reach Liverpool but ended up within sight of the famous waterfront across the river with the Royal Liver Building prominent. Goods were shipped across the river in barges from a basin inside the goods shed to GWR warehouses in Liverpool docks and direct to and from ships in dock or anchored in the river. This goods station was rebuilt in 1929-30, the basin was filled in and the marshalling yard was enlarged to a capacity of 850 wagons, shunted by GWR pannier tank engines, and goods were carried across the river by GWR lorries and vans using Woodside vehicular ferry and later the Mersey road tunnel. The goods station and yard closed in 1972. The adjacent Wallasey Dock was filled in and the whole site is now a waiting area for cars and lorries going aboard a vehicular ferry to Belfast, which berths at a new landing stage on the river wall between Woodside and Seacombe.

Right: **BIRKENHEAD** These two 0-4-0 saddle tank dockside shunting engines, *Glanmor* and *Jessie*, both built in 1907, are pictured on the weed-overgrown sidings at Duke Street Wharf in 1951. They were owned by Cudworth & Johnson of Wrexham and leased to Rea Ltd, ship and tug owners, master porters and stevedores in the export of coal and iron ore from the adjacent wharf. *Glanmor* (right) was built by Hawthorn, Leslie & Company at Newcastle and *Jessie* (left) by Peckett & Sons at Bristol. On the right is a steam coal crane and on the left we see the stern of a cargo-passenger liner at Henderson's Wharf on the far, Wallasey side of the West Float.

BIRKENHEAD Three steam tugs of J. H. Lamey Ltd, Liverpool, are berthed at the former LNWR's Cathcart Street goods station on the East Float, and the floating crane *Mammoth* loads a Clan liner in Vittoria Dock in this general view of dockland on 22 October 1962. *Mammoth*, owned by the Mersey Docks & Harbour Board, was Dutch-built in 1920 with twin smokestacks and a 200-foot jib that could lift up to 200 tons. Cathcart Street warehouse was first used as a hostel for emigrants awaiting passage by sailing 'clippers' from the wharf to the Australian gold rush in the 1850s. The 'Emigrants' Depot', as it was called, opened in 1852 to protect the emigrants from the predatory spivs on Liverpool waterfront. As the docks were extended, Birkenhead exported coal, iron, steel, engineering, pottery, chemicals and railway locomotives and carriages from the industrial hinterland and imported grain, livestock, meat, heavy oil, molasses, timber and iron ore. By 1969 these docks were handling 40 per cent of the tonnage in the port of Liverpool. Today Vittoria Dock is used by mothballed ships and we see very little activity in the other docks between Birkenhead and Wallasey as trade has followed the shift to containerisation in new and larger docks at Bootle and Seaforth on the mouth of the Mersey.

BIRKENHEAD A ship of the Head Line, owned by the Ulster Steamship Company, discharges grain at Joseph Rank's Ocean Flour Mills, built in 1912, on the West Float in August 1954. To the right are Vernon's mill of 1898 and its post-war concrete silo, which stand on the site of the former Canada Works of Thomas Brassey, the world's greatest railway contractor. To the left of Rank's mills is Gill Brook Basin, the site of William Laird's first shipbuilding yard (1828-56) before it moved to the Mersey bank at Tranmere. The picture is framed between a railway goods wagon (left) and the stern of the Ellerman cargo-passenger liner *City of Liverpool* of 1949 on the Wallasey side of the docks. All the mills in dockland between Birkenhead and Wallasey have disappeared and Merseyside's only grain terminal and mill is at the new Seaforth Dock at the river mouth.

Below: **SEACOMBE** The 0-4-0 saddle-tank engine *Cyclops* of 1895 takes water in William Lee's one-road engine shed off Birkenhead Road in 1954; W. J. Lee specialised in general repair work on any dockside locomotives. This engine was built by Hudswell, Clarke at Leeds and worked at Woolwich Arsenal before being bought second-hand and rebuilt by Cudworth & Johnson of Wrexham and leased to Joseph Perrin & Sons Ltd, one of the Birkenhead dockside haulage contractors, based at a shed on Shore Road, Birkenhead. *Cyclops* was used to shunt the Mersey Cattle Wharf at Woodside, the flour mills at Seacombe and other industrial premises in dockland. The pit-prop across the buffer beam was for shunting wagons on an adjacent track! For its size *Cyclops* could haul long trains along the streets and soldiered on with its melodious chime whistle echoing against the mills and warehouses till 1964, when it was scrapped. The double-track dock railway alongside Birkenhead Road served the coaling stage for the steam ferries at Seacombe.

Above: **SEACOMBE** The Rea Towing Company's steam tug *Dongarth* of 1922 leads this procession of cargo-passenger liners through Alfred Dock into the East Float in August 1954. Its towlines are secured to the bow of Alfred Holt's Blue Funnel liner *Polydorus* of 1944. Berthed on the left is the Shaw, Savill & Albion passenger liner *Gothic*, which had been used as a Royal Yacht for Queen Elizabeth and Prince Philip from Jamaica to Australasia and Aden on their tour of the British Commonwealth in 1953-54. Alfred Dock is the vestibule dock to the 2½-mile line of docks between Birkenhead and Wallasey, and the drawbridge on Tower Road has been raised for the passage of the ships entering the docks from the river at high water. Tower Road was a causeway across the docks from Birkenhead to Seacombe, with three drawbridges and one swing bridge that opened for the passage of ships and held up road and rail traffic between the two towns; there was a fifth dock bridge on Spike Road. With the closure of Morpeth and Egerton Docks and the infilling of Wallasey Dock, this drawbridge at Alfred Dock is the only one left on Tower Road, but spectacles like this will never be seen again.

Above: **SEACOMBE** Back in the days when two vessels ran direct between Seacombe and Liverpool, the 1958 TSMV *Royal Daffodil II*, the last tonnage built for Wallasey Corporation Ferries, is seen leaving Seacombe for Liverpool on 26 September 1964 as tugs escort an Ellerman cargo-passenger liner into Alfred Dock to berth in the West Float. The *Daffodil* was built by James Lamont at Port Glasgow, 149 feet by 46 feet, 609 gross tons, and licensed to carry 1,950 passengers. She was sold to Greece in 1977, partly rebuilt to carry vehicles aft on a ferry service out of Piraeus and renamed *Ioulis Keas II*.

Left: **SEACOMBE** Wallasey Corporation buses unload at the ferry terminus in Victoria Place in 1954. Ten bus routes converged on this ferry and the buses were timed to meet the steamers, running every 10 minutes in the peak period and every 15 minutes in the off-peak. Alighting passengers entered under the grand, classical, 1930s Portland stone colonnade and Romanesque arch and walked through the booking hall, with its varnished Art Deco wooden kiosks, and down the bridge to the floating landing stage and the waiting ferry steamer. The bus conductors have already turned their rear destination blinds for the return journeys: 1 to New Brighton via Seabank Road, 4 to Saughall Massie Hotel via Moreton Shore, and 2 to Harrison Drive via Liscard. The buses seen here (from left to right) are two Metropolitan-Cammell/Leylands built in 1946 and 1951 and an 8-foot-wide Weymann-bodied Leyland of 1952.

Below: **SEACOMBE** This picture illustrates the colour scheme of Wallasey Corporation buses and the style of lettering and fleet numerals. The legend 'Wallasey Corporation Motors' was in gold leaf, shaded dark blue with the borough coat of arms in the centre. There were no advertisements till declining revenue saw their advent in 1952. The Metropolitan-Cammell Carriage & Wagon Company, Birmingham, built this style of bus body for Wallasey Corporation from 1937 to 1951 on Leyland and AEC chassis, and this is one of the 1951 stock on Leyland PD2 chassis. Wallasey had a total of 118 buses with this style of Metropolitan-Cammell bodywork and 101 of them were in service when this last batch arrived. The 1951 stock remained in service till 1972-73. Interior features were beige leather seats, French-polished mahogany window frames and beading on the ceilings, and a mock clock dial on the rear bulkhead showing boarding passengers the time of the ferry connection to Liverpool. The photograph was taken at the loading colonnade in Victoria Square at Seacombe ferry in glorious evening sunshine on 15 August 1962, the clock showing 7.25pm. Route 17 was the 'trip round the island', the most circuitous of the five routes from Seacombe to New Brighton, running through Poulton and Wallasey, 5¼ miles against 2¼ miles by the direct route 1.

Above: **SEACOMBE** After unloading at the ferry tollhouse, the buses line up in herringbone order, backing up to the loading colonnade on the south side of Victoria Place as the passengers stream off the ferry. At departure time, the inspector will blow his whistle, all the cab doors will slam in quick succession and the buses will leave together in convoy like elephants nose-to-tail to disperse to all parts of the borough. There were loading bays for 17 buses here, including short workings, on the ten routes that terminated at Seacombe ferry. This picture was taken in 1950 when nearly all the buses were Metropolitan-Cammell-bodied Leylands built in 1937-48. The ferry buildings and bus station were rebuilt in classical red brick and Portland stone in 1930-33 to the design of the borough surveyor, Lionel Wilkinson. Atop the clock tower on the ferry tollhouse is a radar scanner to navigate both Wallasey and Birkenhead ferries in fog. The buildings on the right housed the ferry offices and workshops, a two-storey garage for 200 cars for ferry patrons, the bus inspector's office, a waiting room, a teetotal refreshment room, and a confectionery kiosk. *George Greenwood*

SEACOMBE & EGREMONT railway terminus was sited at the top of Victoria Place by the ferry and bus terminus at Seacombe, but three-quarters of a mile from Egremont. It was one of four obscure LNER railheads on the west coast of Britain, the other three being Southport Lord Street, Silloth and Mallaig. When this picture was taken in 1952 this quiet and lowly station saw only eight passenger trains a day on a route through mid-Wirral to Connah's Quay and Wrexham Central. The last two coaches seen here are ex-Great Central, the nearest dating from 1904. There were also goods trains delivering Welsh coal to coalyards. The Seacombe branch was owned by the Wirral Railway, later part of the LMSR, which ended its Seacombe-West Kirby service in 1938, leaving the LNER to continue running the Seacombe-Wrexham service. The LNER did not own the lines to Seacombe and Southport but had running powers to work the trains, having access over the former Great Central and Cheshire Lines. The Seacombe branch closed to passengers in 1960 and to goods in 1963. Wrexham passenger trains were diverted from Bidston to New Brighton and the trackbed of the Seacombe branch was replaced by the dual-carriageway approach to the second Mersey road tunnel, which opened in 1971. Wrexham trains now terminate at Bidston for connections with the Mersey and Wirral line electric trains.

Below: **POULTON** We meet the dock engine *Cyclops* again on Duke Street, as it runs light between shunting duties towards the drawbridge that divides the East and West Floats and carries one of the three roads across the docks from Birkenhead into Wallasey. Ambling in reverse, the engine is about to overtake a horse and cart. Double tracks ran along the middle of Duke Street from this junction with Dock Road, Poulton, to Corporation Road, Birkenhead, the bridge being the frontier between the two boroughs. Goods trains took their place in the normal order of road traffic on Duke Street, dwarfing private cars and filing closely past buses on the joint cross-docks routes 10, 11 and 12. Buses on these routes were also subject to delays by ships passing the open bridge and by long BR goods trains across Duke Street alongside Corporation Road. The electric drawbridge here replaced a hydraulic swing bridge in 1931. On the right is the dock master's office by the West Float.

Above: **SEACOMBE** Dock Road passed through the canyon of mills by the East Float and here, in 1954, we see a horse-drawn waggon preceding a Birkenhead Corporation bus dropping a passenger at the corner of Oakdale Road. The bus is a 1948 Massey-bodied Leyland on the Birkenhead and Wallasey joint route 12 from Charing Cross to Seacombe Ferry via Park Station. A 1947 Bedford articulated lorry is parked on the left, laden with sacks of flour. Behind it are Paul Brothers' Homepride Mills and beyond are Buchanan's Flour Mills, connected by footbridges, with their animal food mills on the right. Most of these mills have been demolished but a listed granary of 1868 has been converted to flats.

LISCARD & POULTON George, the friendly booking clerk, porter and general factotum at this other station on the Seacombe branch, poses with his luggage trolley of racing pigeon baskets on the up platform. The eaves of the station roof were extended to form a scanty canopy over the platforms. The view is looking west to Breck Road bridge and Bidston Moss. The station and coal siding, off Mill Lane, Poulton, lay in a rock cutting, hewn through the red sandstone of the Wallasey plateau, which deepened as the line passed through Poulton towards Seacombe. Access to this island platform was by a covered, wooden footbridge off the ramp to the coalyard, and trains left this side for Wrexham. The line was popular among Wallaseyans for a day return to rural Wirral stations, to Caergwrle Castle & Wells or Cefn-y-Bedd in Wales (see Part 6) for a walk and a picnic. The station closed to passengers in 1960 and to goods in 1963. Then from 1966 the rock cutting was widened to take a four-lane dual carriageway from the M53 Wirral motorway to the second Mersey road tunnel, from Seacombe to Liverpool, opened in 1971.

NEW BRIGHTON The J. H. Lamey tug *Alfred Lamey*, built in 1908, is seen on the Mersey off New Brighton on a windy 19 September 1964. New Brighton, on the corner of the Mersey and the Irish Sea, was a thriving seaside resort and saw a post-war resurgence in 1948-65. Most of the features we see in the background, the Tower Building, the Tower fairground, the Tivoli Theatre, the ferry pier and the pleasure pier, have all disappeared, but the trees (left) and Perch Rock lighthouse (extreme right) still feature.

   The Tower Building of 1898 stood at the base of a latticed steel tower like Blackpool's but slightly taller and octagonal in plan. It was the tallest structure in Britain when it was completed in 1900, but it closed in 1914 for the Kaiser war, when neglect made it unsafe, and dismantled in 1919-21. The Tower Building that remained housed a theatre and ballroom among the largest in Britain but was gutted by fire and demolished in 1969. Today New Brighton has reverted to its origin as a pleasant residential town for Liverpool businessmen.

Right: **NEW BRIGHTON** Wallasey had a foretaste of the future when the Corporation took delivery of the first production model of Britain's first rear-engine, front-entrance double-deck bus, the Leyland Atlantean, in 1958. Wallasey Atlantean No 1 appeared at that year's Commercial Motor Show at London's Earl's Court and entered service in Wallasey on 8 December. It seated 77 passengers compared with the usual 56 and was easily adapted to one-man operation that resulted from staff shortages and rising costs in the 1970s. Wallasey had 30 Atlanteans, delivered from 1958 to 1961. The plain, rectangular, Metropolitan-Cammell bodies looked neat and smart in Wallasey's yellowy-green and cream colours divided by black beading and with the traditional lettering and fleet numerals on the side panels, but this presentation was changed under new management from 1961. No 9 was new when pictured in Virginia Road bus station, New Brighton, on 11 May 1960, loading for route 1 to Seacombe via Seabank Road. The Mark 1 Atlanteans served Wallasey till 1979 but this is still the basic design of modern double-deckers on the road today.

Leftt: **GREASBY** Coke-fired steam lorries dating from the 1920s and '30s were still at work in the mid-20th century, and Liverpool dockland was their last stronghold. The Sentinel Waggon Works of Shrewsbury went on building steam lorries until 1950 and maintained a service depot at Duke's Dock, Liverpool, until 1957. The last steam lorry there worked between the mills and the docks in 1962. This Sentinel steam tar sprayer, dating from 1929, pictured working on Frankby Road, Greasby, in September 1954, was the last steam road locomotive in commercial use in Britain, working until 1984. It was a Sentinel DG4P: a double-geared (two-speed) four-wheeler on pneumatic tyres. It had a vertical boiler and chimney at the front of the cab, the engine slung under the chassis and chain drive (with two giant bicycle-type chains) to the back axle. It was built as a flatbed lorry for a Birmingham brickworks and was sold in 1942 to a Chester mineral water company. In 1944 Robert Bridson & Son, contractors, of Neston, converted it to a tar sprayer with a tar boiler on the back platform, heated by steam from the boiler in the cab; a small steam pump, spray bar and hand lance were fitted at the back. It worked on Wirral roads till 1968 and moved on to Lloyd-Jones Brothers of Ruthin, spraying Denbighshire roads until 1984, when it was retired. It languished till 1997, when it was sold for preservation. It is now restored to full working order and runs on steam rallies.

WEST KIRBY Outside the railway terminus (right) on Grange Road in September 1954 are two Wolseley taxicabs of 1937-39, a girl riding a bicycle with a basket on the front, and a 1949 Morris Isis car, with its bowed radiator and two-piece windscreen, rounding the bend from Meols Drive. A 1952 Hillman Minx car is parked on the left and a boy on a scooter pauses before crossing the road. The railway station was rebuilt in 1896 at the western terminus of the Wirral Railway from Birkenhead, electrified by the LMSR in 1938. Beyond the station, the Edwardian baroque Barclay's Bank in red sandstone, on the corner of Meols Drive and Dee Lane, terminates the view.

WEST KIRBY The Crescent was the shopping centre of town and on this day in September 1954 we see, parked on the left, a 1931 Morris 8 car and a 1948 Austin A40 van, while on the right is a 1953 Rover 75 car. Today the iron and glass colonnade and the canvas sun blinds have disappeared and the buildings with the decorative timber framework that terminate the view have been replaced with stark, modern blocks. The shopping centre has moved to a supermarket in Dee Lane.

Index of locations

The Transport Travelogue series *(Volume numbers shown refer to the Recollections series numbering)*

Vol 70: A Transport Travelogue by road rail and water, 1948-1972
Part 1, South-east England: Kent, London and Sussex

July 2018		By Cedric Greenwood
169 x 238mm	64pp	c60col/b&w
ISBN: 978 1 85794 503 4	Softcover	£8.00

Vol 71: A Transport Travelogue by road rail and water, 1948-1972
Part 2, South and South West England: Wessex to Cornwall

July 2018		By Cedric Greenwood
169 x 238mm	48pp	c60col/b&w
ISBN: 978 1 85794 502 7	Softcover	£6.00

Vol 72: A Transport Travelogue by road rail and water, 1948-1972
Part 3, Eastern and Midland Counties: Norfolk to Cheshire

July 2018		By Cedric Greenwood
169 x 238mm	64pp	c60col/b&w
ISBN: 978 1 85794 504 1	Softcover	£8.00

Vol 73: A Transport Travelogue by road rail and water, 1948-1972
Part 4, Lancashire: Widnes to Furness

July 2018		By Cedric Greenwood
169 x 238mm	64pp	c60col/b&w
ISBN: 978 1 85794 499 0	Softcover	£8.00

Vol 74: A Transport Travelogue by road rail and water, 1948-1972
Part 5, Yorkshire to the Border

July 2018		By Cedric Greenwood
169 x 238mm	64pp	c60col/b&w
ISBN: 978 1 85794 501 0	Softcover	£8.00

Vol 94: A Transport Travelogue by road rail and water, 1948-1972
Part 6, Wales, Man and Scotland

July 2018		By Cedric Greenwood
169 x 238mm	64pp	c60col/b&w
ISBN: 978 1 85794 500 3	Softcover	£8.00